RALPH,

CONGRATS ON RETIREMENT!

WELL EARNED MY FRIEND..

PLENTY OF TIME FOR GOLF.

Stu Ward

MAY 2017

The *New* Why Book of Golf

William C. Kroen

BARNES
&NOBLE
BOOKS
NEW YORK

1999 Barnes & Noble Books

Book design by Lundquist Design, New York

ISBN 0-7607-1497-5

Printed and bound in the United States of America

99 00 01 02 03 MC 9 8 7 6 5 4 3 2 1

RRD-H

To the members of the
Furnace Brook Golf Club

The Contents

The Game

Mark Twain called it "a good walk spoiled." Some twenty million Americans are locked into a love-hate relationship with it. We spend over a billion dollars per year on equipment alone; we study videotapes and read texts as if learning brain surgery; we hunch toward the TV as the announcer whispers in the common language of all who play the game. How did this national obsession come about? What is the history of this distinctive game?

Golf's true origin is as hazy as ancient history. It was the Scots, however, who organized the game on a playing field, gave it rules and provided the vocabulary that we so often use today in our Sunday foursomes. Whether it was a shepherd hitting stones with his staff or sailors knocking stones along the path to the town with a club, the glorious game as it has evolved is rich in tradition and lore. The things we say and do on the golf course often have deep roots, and knowing the history can add to our overall enjoyment of the great game of golf.

Why is golf so named?

The word "golf" comes from the German word *kolbe,* which means club. The name has been used for many games played with clubs (the Dutch game *kolven,* for example). A debate about the origin of golf has been ongoing: Did it begin with the Flemish game of *chole,* the French *jeu de mail* or the Roman game of *Paganica* (the game of countrymen)? No one knows. The Scots, however, were the first to play the game of golf as it is played today. The first recorded reference to golf came in an Act of Scottish Parliament in 1457 that forbade golf and "futeball" because Scotland was at war with England, and the government didn't want young men neglecting military training.

Why are sand traps called "bunkers"?

"Bunker" comes from the Scottish *bonker,* meaning a chest or box where coal is kept, usually dug into the side of a hill. Often, cows would graze in the marshlands adjacent to the old links courses, standing alongside the dunes and creating a depression that reminded Scottish players of these chests, and eventually these areas became known as bunkers.

Why is the word "bogey" used to describe a score of one over par?

The term comes from an imaginary Colonel Bogey of the Great Yarmouth Club in England. It is believed that a Major Charles Wellman, while playing against ground score (par), referred to failing to get par as "getting caught by the bogey man," a phrase from a popular eighteenth-century tune. The members of the club began referring to an imaginary new member, Colonel Bogey, who would always shoot even par. As the game spread to the United States, "bogey" was narrowed to represent a score of one over par on a hole.

Why is the word "birdie" used for a score of one under par on a hole?

According to *Golf Magazine's Encyclopedia of Golf,* "birdie" was coined in the United States. In 1903 a certain A. H. Smith of Atlantic City is said to have remarked after holing out, "That's a bird of a shot!" The words "eagle" and "double eagle" are outgrowths of the bird reference.

Why are the spectators at a golf tournament called a "gallery"?

In British theaters the large balcony containing the cheaper seats is called a gallery. Over the years the term has come to signify the public in general.

Why is the Masters considered one of the Grand Slam tournaments?

The Masters is the only privately run tournament of the big four considered to be the Grand Slam of golf. The U.S. Open, the PGA Championship and the British Open are all run and sanctioned by national golf institutions. The Masters has attained its prestigious place in golf history and lore with a great course, excellent ambience, exclusiveness, tradition and careful promotion. Bobby Jones started the Masters in 1934 as a starting tournament for the pro tour as the pros headed north after the winter season in Florida. Jones was interested in showcasing his Augusta National Course by having the greatest players available test their games each spring as the magnolias blossomed. By invitation only, the Masters provides an atmosphere free of commercialism and dedicated to the art of golf. Clifford Roberts, who ran the tournament from the thirties right up to 1980, maintained an elite aura in every respect of the tournament, from television coverage to clubhouse decorum. The Masters grew in respect and esteem over the years to its current position as one of the most coveted titles in the game.

Why are some tournaments called "opens"?

"Open" means that the tournament is open to both amateurs and professionals.

Why and how is par assigned to a hole?

Par is the score that an expert golfer should make on that particular hole; it is set in order to have a standard against which to measure score and determine handicaps. Par is generally based on the length of the hole, but allowances are made for level of difficulty caused by terrain features. The USGA's guidelines for par according to distance are:

Par	Men	Women
3	up to 250	up to 210
4	251 to 470	211 to 400
5	over 470	401 to 575

Why is four the accepted number of golfers for one group?

In its earliest form, golf was strictly match play in format, and four is the smallest number of players for team matches. As a result, competition between clubs in England and America in the nineteenth century was always in the foursome grouping. Even as the format changed, however, numbers greater than four were generally frowned upon because they slowed down the game and caused confusion around the green.

Why is it considered bad form to walk across someone's line before he or she putts?

There are two main reasons why this breach of etiquette is considered serious. Firstly, by walking on someone's line, you may leave an indentation that could affect the roll of the putt. Secondly, the intrusion across a player's line may cause a break in the player's concentration. Most good players try to visualize the line of the putt as they are sizing it up. Walking across that line disturbs that visual picture.

In the early days of golf, why were feathers used as stuffing for golf balls?

The old "featheries" were surprisingly alive. A large amount of chicken feathers was boiled and then stuffed firmly into a leather cover. When the feathers dried and expanded they stretched the leather so it became quite resilient. The ball actually went a good distance, with drives of over 300 yards recorded, but the ball was phased out about 1850.

Why is a game of golf referred to as a "round"?

In the early days of golf, all courses were constructed in a circular fashion. The first hole was near the clubhouse, and the other holes would circle through the countryside, coming back to the starting point on the eighteenth hole.

Why is the word "divot" used to describe a piece of earth dislodged by a club stroke?

"Divot" is a Scottish word for a piece of turf.

Why is the tradition of "having the honor"—allowing the player who scored the lowest on the previous hole to tee off first—used, and what, if any, advantage does it bestow?

Having the honor is part of the rules, establishing a uniform system of order for playing first off the tee. To hit first can be a distinct advantage, as a good shot may put pressure on an opponent.

Why is the overlapping grip sometimes called the "Vardon"?

Harry Vardon, who won the British Open six times and the U.S. Open once, was a great promoter and golfer at the turn of the century. He was often photographed using the overlap grip. He is not, however, considered to be the inventor of the grip, as several well-known players, including Leslie Balfour Melville and J. H. Taylor, had used the grip successfully before Vardon reached fame as a golfer.

THE *NEW* WHY BOOK OF GOLF

Why is the higher side of a cup on an incline called "the pro side"?

A good player will read the break of a putt correctly, allowing enough break and putting to the higher side. The lower side of the hole is sometimes called "the sucker's side" because the poor golfer will not read the break correctly.

Why are golf courses sometimes called "links"?

According to Webster Evans's *Encyclopedia of Golf* the word is derived from Old English *hlinc,* meaning ridge of land. Links land is gently undulating land, often running along the seashore. In the strict sense of the term, a links golf course should be one that borders the sea.

Why is a golfer who averages par referred to as a "scratch" player?

The Standard Scratch and Handicapping Scheme developed by the Council of National Golf Unions devised a system of comparing golf courses based on length. The score that was deemed its true par (much as courses are rated today) was called the "scratch score." A player who averaged scratch score was called a scratch man.

Why is "nassau" used to describe a match played on both nines and an overall eighteen?

A nassau bet sets up three separate matches: the front nine, the back nine and the entire eighteen holes. When a player or side goes down by two holes, a "press" can be made. A press doubles the amount of the bet and creates a new match for the number of holes remaining. This popular form of match comes from a betting practice that was very popular in the Caribbean Islands. The practice spread to the United States where it has become a standard form of betting in most clubs.

Why is the term "dormie" used when someone is ahead by the same number of holes left in the match?

"Dormie" probably comes from the Latin *dormire* "to sleep." "The player who is ahead cannot lose though he go to sleep."

Why is the word "putt" used in golf?

Putt comes from the word "put." Once on the green, the object of that particular stroke is to "put" the ball into the hole.

Why has golf become so popular?

It is estimated that there are over twenty million golfers in the United States alone, with a growth rate that will add one to two million golfers per year over the next ten years. Sixty percent of new golfers are women. There are several reasons for the boom. The baby boom generation, now at middle age, has found golf to be a recreation of the successful business executive. According to the National Golf Foundation 67 percent of business executives play the game; it is more than a cliché that many business transactions take place on a golf course. Compared to other adult games, golf offers many unique characteristics. As all holes and courses are different, the player is constantly faced with unique situations that require strategic decisions that are relatively scarce in other sports.

The game is very difficult to master and offers a real challenge, appealing to many success-oriented people. The Japanese, who have a long history of being fascinated by very challenging games such as Go and the martial arts, have been taking up the game of golf in huge numbers despite the lack of courses. Several million golfers in Japan may never play on a real course, accepting golf's challenge solely on the driving range.

The game does not require size, strength or particularly outstanding athletic ability but emphasizes such attributes as tempo, concentration, strategy and accuracy. Combine the intrinsic elements of golf's lure with sunshine, fresh air and moderate exercise, and it becomes clear why the love affair has grown.

As A. A. Milne once said, "Golf is popular simply because it is the best game at which to be bad."

Why is the Ryder Cup match so named?

The Ryder Cup matches are played between American PGA professionals and pros from Europe every two years. An unofficial match between the U.S. and England played in Surrey, England, in 1926 prompted the tradition; the match was very popular and a wealthy seed merchant named Samuel Ryder presented a gold cup at the first official match at Worcester, Massachusetts, in 1927, with the American team winning.

Why is the term "bye" used when a player does not have an opponent in a match?

The term "bye" probably started as a farewell to someone who had lost a match 10 and 8 in an eighteen-hole match. Not having to play the remaining holes, an opponent in this situation also had a "bye," and gradually the term was extended to anyone who did not have to play a match.

Why does "fairway" describe the close-cut part of a course?

The Rules of Golf do not specifically define the word "fairway" but generally refer to it as "through the green." In early references to the game, the playing area was often called the "fair green." As time went on, the term "fairway," as opposed to the "rough," became most common.

Why is the term "mulligan" used for the granting of a second chance at a drive on the first hole?

The origin of "mulligan" is not clear, but it may be rhyming slang for "have at it again."

Why is a very poor round of golf sometimes referred to as "military golf"?

A hacker having an extremely wild day off the tee calls to mind a drill sergeant's cadence call: "Left-right-left-right!"

Why is a "skins" competition so named?

In a "skins" game players compete on each hole, the player with the lowest score winning a "skin." The term goes back to the days when a hunter would display his success by the number of pelts or skins he had upon returning from the hunt.

Why is the phrase "rub of the green" used to describe any odd or accidental occurrence in the game of golf?

The 1812 code of the Royal and Ancient Golf Committee used the following expression in Rule IX: "Whatever happens to a ball by accident must be reckoned a rub of the green." "Rub" here means a hindrance or difficulty (as in the Elizabethan phrase "there's the rub"), and "green" is a common term for the whole course.

Why is the word "stymie" used in golf?

The word "stymie" comes from the Scottish word *styme,* meaning a person who is partially blind. In golf, stymie rules used to allow a golfer to putt his ball onto the line of his opponent in order to block the path to the hole. If you were stymied, you could not "see" the hole. Stymies were taken out of the Rules in 1952 as they tended to lessen the importance of true golfing skill and slow the game down. Today, "stymied" is used by golfers to describe a situation where they are blocked along their line to the green by an obstacle such as a tree or large rock.

Why do golfers tend to dress in very colorful attire?

The tradition of bright clothing goes back to the very beginnings of the game. Archers would wear bright red uniforms for much the same reason hunters wear orange and red today. As the early clubs were often made up of mostly military men, the idea of wearing bright clothing in order to be seen while playing carried over to the game of golf.

Why do many instructional books equate an "average" golfer with a poor one?

Golf is a very difficult game to master. According to the National Golf Foundation, the average golfer will shoot in the high 90s on a par 72 course. Only one player in twelve will break eighty with any consistency. The practice, experience, knowledge and athletic ability needed to play golf is well beyond the level possible for the "average" golfer.

Why is the term "Grand Slam" used to describe winning the U.S. Open, British Open, PGA Championship and the Masters?

"Grand Slam," with its baseball meaning obviously in mind, was first used in golf to describe Bobby Jones's amazing feat in 1930 of winning the U.S. and British Opens and the national amateur championships of both countries. With the lessening in importance of amateur play, the phrase eventually arrived at its modern meaning.

Why is three under par on one hole sometimes referred to as an "albatross"?

"Albatross" is simply an extension of birdie and eagle and like them is considered an American term. The word never really caught on among golfers, however, and the term "double eagle" has generally replaced it in modern golf vernacular.

Why is the handicap system often used at amateur net tournaments called the "Callaway System"?

In 1957 Lionel F. Callaway invented a system that yields instant handicaps based on the round shot. The system is used extensively when large numbers of competitors who do not have handicaps play. The system eliminates the worst score of the round in descending order based on the total score for the day.

Why is the Walker Cup so named?

The Walker Cup matches are played between the top amateurs from the United States and Great Britain. The Cup began with an unofficial match the day before the British Amateur Championship in 1921. George H. Walker, president of the United States Golf Association, had agreed to provide a cup for the winning team starting in 1922. The newspapers quickly referred to it as the Walker Cup and the name stuck.

Why is the Curtis Cup so named?

The Curtis Cup matches are played between the top women amateurs from the United States and Great Britain every two years. An unofficial competition, begun in 1905 between the two countries, steadily grew in popularity until it was decided to begin an official event in 1932. Two sisters, Margaret and Harriet Curtis, had played in many of the unofficial matches and offered to donate a cup for the competition. The Curtis sisters had won four USGA Ladies' Championships between them at the time.

Why do golfers yell "fore!" to warn others of an approaching shot?

Most experts think the term derives from a warning used by the British Army in battle, which formed ranks of infantry at the front with artillery located to the rear. Before firing a volley, the artillery yelled "beware before" to the infantry, who then lay down to let the cannonballs fly overhead. Shortened to "fore," the term eventually came to be used by golfers to warn other players of a missile headed their way.

Why are there eighteen holes?

The number of holes on a golf course was not fixed until the eighteenth century. In 1764 the Royal and Ancient Golf Club reduced its number of holes from twenty-two to eighteen by combining eight of them into four. As legislation on the Rules was being written at the same time, eighteen was agreed upon by common consent.

Why is the term "caddy" used in golf, and what is its history?

The word probably comes from the French word cadet, meaning "young man." Mary Queen of Scots, an avid golfer, used the young men of her court to carry her clubs. The word had been adopted by the Scottish to refer to a porter or someone who does odd jobs, but partly because of Mary's use "caddy" was gradually applied to the young men who did the various jobs as greenskeeper, club repairer and ballmarker around the course before narrowing in meaning to its present use.

Why is stroke play called "medal play"?

In the early days of golf in England and Scotland, there were no trophies given to the winners of club championships. Instead, a medal was given to the winner, and he was bestowed with the title of "Captain" for one year. The medals are now considered very valuable among golf collectors.

Why are hollows or small streams on Scotland's courses called "burns"?

The small streams that run across and through the courses of Scotland become water hazards. It was said that players who hit their balls into them "got burned" by them.

Why is the name "Stableford" given to a point scoring system that is used on one PGA Tour event?

The name comes from The Stableford Club in Yorkshire, England, where it is alleged to have started by its members. In Stableford scoring, five points are awarded for an eagle, three for a birdie, and one for a par. Subtractions are made for scores over par. The PGA Tour plays a modified version of the Stableford.

Why is the term "fore caddie" given to one who goes out on a hole to spot drives for players?

In the early days of golf, the game was played through public areas where women, children and others would be strolling. The job of the "fore caddie" was to run ahead of the golfers yelling "fore" to warn people that golfers were coming, and to be watchful of flying balls.

Why are the Irish rebellion and golf intertwined in British history?

King Charles I became a golf fanatic during his reign. He was harshly criticized and forced to forfeit his crown because he neglected his duties, allowing the Rebellion to take shape while he was so often out playing golf. He actually received the news of the Irish uprising while on the course.

Why was there a rift between the governing bodies of Britain and the United States that lasted for years?

Essentially, it was mistrust. As golf began to take hold in the United States at the end of the 19th century, the British took a worried view of what would happen to the game once Americans started playing. America was noted for it's innovation, technology and free ideas. However, in golf, the British felt that the Americans would change the Rules, and that American courses would not be built like the links courses in England. In 1897, H. J. Whigham wrote, "It is certain that before long the American golfers, who are not bound hand and foot by tradition will introduce one or two remedial measures (to the Rules) which will incense conservative Britain."

The Equipment

The evolution of golf equipment traces the game's history and chronicles the never-ending search for the perfect match between man and tool. Watch a golf junkie in a pro shop as he works his way through a rack of putters. Suddenly, he holds one in front of him as the thousand-yard stare tells us, "Yes, this is it! This is the one that will change my golfing life!" Men who cannot explain the function of a carburetor can explain how swingweight and torque are related in the shaft of a 2-iron.

From the early featheries to aerodynamically designed dimple patterns, golf-ball technology has evolved steadily. Clubs have gone from crude wooden sticks to finely crafted instruments of boron or titanium. Golfers of all ages engage in love affairs with their equipment in the search for the perfect tools.

Why does a golf ball have dimples?

The primary function of dimples is to provide lift. As the ball spins off the club, the tiny cups trap air in such a way that the air moves more quickly over the top of the ball than around the bottom, causing the ball to rise. This aerodynamic principle is the same as the one that causes airplanes to lift off the ground.

Why does a golf club have grooves?

The grooves on a club stop the ball from sliding up the clubface at impact. As a ball is struck, it will ride up on the clubface until the grooves and dimples of the ball interact to trap the ball and help propel it forward. The grooves also create backspin which allows the ball to take flight.

Why do some putters have grips that are flat on the top?

Under the Rules of Golf (4-1c) putters are the only clubs that can have such grips. The purpose of the flat grip is to accommodate the most common putting grip, which places both thumbs directly down the middle of the shaft. This grip helps prevent the hands from rolling and thus throwing the ball off line.

Why are wood clubs rounded on the face instead of flat from heel to toe?

This feature is called "bulge." The slight curve from heel to toe actually helps shots that are mishit. A ball struck on the toe, for example, will fly off to the right, but the bulge on the clubface will give it a counterclockwise spin, causing it to hook back toward the center of the fairway. A ball struck on the heel will react in the opposite manner.

Why are the spikes on golf shoes so arranged?

The proper golf swing requires that a golfer maintain good balance while shifting weight from one foot to the other. The spikes on most golf shoes are placed so that they line the outsides of both the heel and sole areas. This design allows the golfer to push off the back foot on the downswing, with his front foot receiving the weight transfer without slipping forward at impact and beyond.

Why aren't golf balls numbered higher—such as 9, 10 or 11?

In the late fifties and early sixties, several golf ball manufacturers did number balls into the double figures. Touring pros, out of superstition, tended to only use low-numbered balls, those numbered 1 through 3 in particular. The everyday golfer soon picked up on the practice and the manufacturers adjusted accordingly.

Why do golfers wear only one glove?

With most grips used today, the left hand (for righthanders) has far more contact with the club. In the Vardon overlapping grip, for example, the entire left hand is placed on the club, while only parts of the first three fingers of the right come into contact with it. While it affords better gripping action for the left hand, a glove would inhibit the function of the right, which is to "feel" and control the clubface.

Why do some wood clubs have a small bulge on the bottom of the club where the shaft ends?

If you are able to see the tip of the shaft on the bottom of the club then this is a "through-bore" club, in which the shaft penetrates all the way through to where the tip is exposed. If the tip is not exposed then the club is said to be a "blind bore." The design changes mainly deal with the flex characteristics of the type of shaft used. Through-bore models tend to handle stiff shaft characteristics better for most steel shafts, but the difference is minor as flex can be controlled by the shaft itself.

Why are some new clubs featuring "offset" as a game-improvement aid?

An offset club is one in which the clubface is set back from the hosel, a design feature that allows the golfer to set up for the shot with his hands in front of the ball and promotes a swing that hits down on the ball. Offset woods help the player eliminate slices as well.

Why is a sand wedge designed differently from other clubs?

A sand wedge is specifically designed to slide under the ball through the sand. The back of the flange or bottom of the club is lower than the front or lead edge of the club. This design feature, called "bounce," allows the club to pass through the sand without becoming buried. In a sand shot, the clubface never actually touches the ball; the concussion of the club striking the sand actually causes the ball to fly up and out of the trap.

Why did wood clubs have tightly wound string around the neck of the club?

Called "whipping," the tightly wound twine served to reinforce the joint where the shaft meets the clubhead. Without this reinforcement the wood near the neck would crack and split from the force of the swing. Today, various materials are used instead of whipping to reinforce the joint.

Why are some clubs curved on the bottom and advertised as "radiused"?

"Radiused," "cambered" or "rocker-soled" clubs are curved from heel to toe to enable the average golfer to make more solid contact from various lies. With a curved sole, only a small part of the leading edge of the club comes into contact with the turf. A radiused club is particularly advantageous for lies on hard pan, or where fairways are dry and grass is sparse.

Why are some wood clubs said to be "persimmon"?

Persimmon is a term used for trees that belong to the ebony family, which have fine, hard wood. In golf, a persimmon wood is one that is made from a solid block of wood. In contrast, a wood club made from gluing layers of wood together is called "laminated." Metal woods are sometimes referred to as "Pittsburgh Persimmon."

Why have some manufacturers started using titanium in their shafts?

Titanium, famous for its use in aircrafts, is lighter than steel and has excellent properties of flex and torque. The lightness of titanium shafts creates a lower center of gravity. Because of this shift in weight, the club can be swung easily and still generate good clubhead speed because the new weighting characteristic keeps the "kick" in the shaft. The one drawback is expense as titanium carries a high price take because of the process needed to develop it.

Why are golf grips tapered from top to bottom when the grips of tennis rackets, fishing rods and baseball bats, for example, are either straight or tapered upwards?

There are several reasons for the shape of the golf grip. Firstly, the shaft of a golf club must taper from top to bottom to flex properly for the golf swing. Also, the golf grip places the two hands closely together so that the meat of the hands is at the top and the fingers at the bottom. Finally, the tapering of the grip allows greater freedom of wrist action, vital to the proper golf swing.

Why are manufacturers using metal in the construction of "woods"?

The metal woods offer the opportunity to create different weight characteristics that can help a golf game. Perimeter weighting, for example, placing weight around the perimeter of the clubface, reduces the amount of twisting at impact. This feature, theoretically, should cause off-center hits to fly straighter.

Why is the word "tee" used for the wooden peg that holds the ball?

The word "tee" probably comes from the Scottish *teay*, a small pile of sand. For many years golfers would make a pile of sand or dirt and place their ball on top of it for driving. In 1920 Dr. William Lowell, a Boston dentist, invented the wooden tee to prevent his hands from becoming scratched.

Why are the clubfaces of woods rounded from top to bottom?

It is mostly a matter of appearance and optics. The clubface is rounded from top to bottom to give the appearance of loft. If the face were cut straight from top to bottom, it would appear almost vertical to the golfer. By rounding, or creating "roll," golf manufacturers are actually helping golfers' confidence in getting the ball into the air.

Why were the earlier models of golf balls called "gutta-percha"?

"Gutta-percha" is a material tapped from several species of Malaysian trees. It resembles rubber but contains more resin and hardens when exposed to air. Golf legend has it that a professor at St. Andrews University received a statue of Vishnu packed in gutta-percha. An avid golfer, the professor rolled the material and tried it out as a golf ball. The ball did not fly very well at first, but as it became more roughed up it started to rise higher. The idea of dimples (to provide lift) thus came into being. Early golf ball craftsmen would place the dimples by hand; later molds were made to produce the early versions of the ball we use today.

Why are some clubs featuring "cavity back" designs?

"Cavity back" clubs are usually investment clubs with a hollowed-out area directly behind the hitting area. This design feature allows club-makers to place additional weight in the heel and toe areas and consequently help the golfer hit straighter shots from off-center hits.

Why do some club manufacturers refer to a "moment of inertia" in describing the characteristics of their clubs?

The moment of inertia is the measure of any object's inertial resistance to turning. The moment of inertia is related to weight and the distribution of weight of the object to be turned. In the clubface, a perimeter weighting or heel-toe weighting design will help prevent twisting by increasing the moment of inertia when shots are hit slightly off of the sweet spot.

Why do many golf ball companies feature such numbers as 382 and 384 on their balls?

The numbers refer to the number of dimples on the ball. The dimples are arranged in certain patterns to produce desired flight characteristics. For example, Maxfli's DDH design is an arrangement of dimples in a dodecahedron pattern that promotes lift and carry in a stabilized flight.

Why do golf balls have compression ratings of 80, 90 and 100?

The compression ratings of 80 (soft), 90 (medium) and 100 (hard) measure the technical concept of "coefficient or restitution," which refers to a ball's ability to spring back into shape after being struck. Tests have shown that the higher the compression the farther the ball will go, regardless of the force of the swing. The soft and medium compression balls are favored by many players because they offer a better feel. Compression is measured by the tightness of the windings or the density of the material in the two-piece ball. Most women use an 80 compression; big hitters and top players use the 100; and the vast majority of all other golfers play with the 90.

Why are tees still made of wood instead of more durable materials?

Tees have been made of wood for over sixty years for several reasons. Firstly, tees made of metal and plastic can scratch and damage wood clubs. The cost of wooden tees has remained very low, and the supply is plentiful. Of course, as with most things in the game of golf, there is tradition. Many top players would never dream of playing with anything but a wooden tee, and the vast majority use white ones only.

Why were aluminum shafts phased out?

Aluminum proved to be too soft for golf shafts, unable to take the tremendous torque and flex involved in the golf swing. Players using aluminum in the late sixties found that the sound at impact was muffled and the distance off the tee quite reduced.

Why is the USGA's robot used for testing golf balls and clubs called "Iron Byron"?

Iron Byron was actually modeled after the swing of Byron Nelson. The USGA wanted a robot that would replicate a near-perfect golf swing based on the swing plane, arc and height of an average-sized man. Nelson's swing, considered to be a classic example of the proper golf swing, was used to set the baseline data for the robot to emulate.

Why, in the early days of golf, were clubs given names such as "niblick" and "mashie"?

Up until the first half of the twentieth century, golf clubs were sold individually. A golfer would look through a batch of mid-irons until he found the right mashie. As a marketing device, club manufacturers created matched sets of clubs. With the onset of matched sets, the system of numbering clubs came into use instead of individual names for each club.

Why were the knickers that golfers used to wear called "plus fours"?

In order to create the effect of pants bloused just below the knee, manufacturers added four inches to the normal length of short pants. Thus the length of the knickers was normal length plus four inches.

Why are Ping clubs so named?

Karsten Solheim, founder of Ping clubs and Karsten Manufacturing, made his first putter on his workbench. The putter was intended to be lightweight and feature heel- and toe-weighing. When Solheim tried it for the first time he was surprised to hear a rather pronounced *ping!* when he struck the putt. Thus the Ping was born. The first putter was not successful, but subsequent models made an impression on the touring pros and soon the business boomed.

Why is the grain in persimmon woods important?

Most golf-club mavens look for a matching grain pattern through all the wood clubs as a sign of careful craftsmanship and matching stocks of wood.

Why were early clubs referred to as "spoons"?

In the early days of golf, clubs that are now called irons were made with spoonlike concave faces. The clubs had specific names such as the "long spoon," "mid-spoon" and "baffing spoon" depending on their use. With the advent of matched, numbered club sets, this term fell from use.

Why was there once a difference between the size of golf balls used in Great Britain and the U.S.?

The difference in size (U.S. 1.68 inches, G.B. 1.62) goes back to 1931, when American manufacturers began making balls slightly larger than the standard British ball. In 1931 the USGA approved the 1.68 diameter as the standard for golf competition. The Royal and Ancient Golf Committee did not go along with the change, and the two countries played with different-sized balls. In 1990, however, the ball was standardized at 1.68 throughout the world, as the R and A agreed to the new standard for play.

Why do grips come in different thicknesses?

The grip differences come in increments of 1/32 of an inch and may have an effect on the swing. Thicker grips tend to restrict wrist and hand action and can help to prevent hooking. On the other hand, thinner grips promote greater hand and wrist action and can help cure a slice.

Why is the term "swingweight" used? Why don't manufacturers just call it the weight of the club?

"Swingweight" is a measure of the club's weight distribution based on a balance point between the head and end of the grip. The overall weight of a club is called the static weight.

Why and how is a "Stimpmeter" used in golf?

A Stimpmeter is a grooved bar used to measure the speed of greens. A ball is placed on the bar, which is raised until the ball rolls freely. The distance that the ball rolls is measured and the operation is repeated several times, with an average being taken. The speed of a green is important to ensure consistency and to create conditions that are considered to be of championship caliber.

Why do some manufacturers use beryllium copper on clubheads?

Beryllium copper adds weight to the clubhead, cuts down on glare and allows the grooves to be cut more sharply into the clubface.

Why is a putter used from off the green called a "Texas wedge"?

Many players from Texas used this technique because of the tough wind conditions there. Using a putter keeps the shots low and the wind's influence minimal. Ben Hogan popularized the technique and the term in the 1950s.

Why do shafts come in different flexes?

Most club manufacturers make four flexes for their shafts. Generally, the type of flex depends on the amount of force exerted on the swing. A powerful swing requires a shaft with little flex in it, as the force of the swing would cause a whippy shaft to bend too much so that the clubhead would strike the ball too soon in the player's swing. Additionally, the clubhead would twist as it reached impact, causing a severe hook. On the other hand, a player who swings easily needs a more flexible shaft in order to have some "kick" or benefit from the shaft bending as a result of centrifugal force. The four standard flexes are:

X-Stiff	— Very powerful swing
Stiff	— Strong player
Regular	— Normal swing, average player
Soft	— Very slow swing

Why are some irons referred to as "muscle back"?

The term "muscle back" refers to forged irons that have bulges or ripples on the back of the clubhead opposite the hitting area. The muscleback iron creates mass near the hitting zone, for additional power.

Why is the word "Modulus" used on graphite shafts?

Modulus is a measure of stiffness. A high modulus shaft would have little flex while low modulus would be more whippy.

Why did early putters have quite an amount of loft?

In the first half of the twentieth century, greens were kept much longer than the greens of today. In order to get the ball up and rolling on the green, the player had to hit a putt that would often resemble a chip shot of today.

Why are diamonds being used in clubs?

Some manufacturers have gone to using industrial grade diamond dust as a coating on wedges to create a rough surface for greater backspin. The diamonds have a much longer life than previous rough surfaces such as plastics and sandblasting.

Why are some manufacturers using titanium in their golf balls?

The use of metals mixed into the golf ball's materials is said to strengthen the material to enable the ball to stay round and to recover from impact. Manufacturers also say that it enables them to help keep the ball balanced for better flight by distributing the weight of the metal throughout the ball.

Why are titanium irons so large?

Titanium is a very lightweight metal—it is often used in air-crafts because of this. When club manufacturers created irons made solely of titanium they had to make the clubhead very large, just to give it a swingweight that would be comfortable to most golfers. If they made the clubhead at normal size, the club would feel too light.

Why are many manufacturers adding inserts to their putters?

The inserts made of materials, from Teflon to copper, offer a softer feel for the player as the ball makes contact with the putter face. While minute, players think that the softer feel enables them to hit putts at the correct speed rather than have the ball seem to bounce off the putter face too quickly.

Why are touring professionals' irons de-lofted or "strong" as opposed to what is sold and used by most golfers?

Because touring professionals generate such great swing speed, the ball would tend to fly extremely high because of the backspin generated on the ball. The tour professionals usually have less loft in their irons than the vast majority of golfers. This, in part, may explain why you see a pro hitting a seven iron 170 yards.

Why is the USGA concerned with something called the "trampoline effect"?

Under Rule 4-i, there can be no parts of the clubhead that are moveable. While the "trampoline effect" is never mentioned in the Rules of Golf, it refers to thin-walled metal woods that may cave in on impact with a ball then spring forward to help propel it off of the clubface. The USGA said that there were no non-complying clubs as of 1999 but they planned to test clubs that are submitted for approval.

Why are club manufacturers touring inserts that provide a low center of gravity?

Golf club makers have found that the average golfer has difficulty getting fairway woods and long irons up into the air on a consistent basis. By placing weight on the bottom of these clubs, the clubhead stays low through impact and allows the ball to be hit a little higher on the clubface and thus propels the ball upward more easily.

The Swing

None of man's movement has been more analyzed, filmed, written about and debated than the golf swing. The search for the perfect golf swing drives us to read about such things as a "power arc" with the intensity of a cardiologist reading an EKG. But the sad truth is that while there are proven principles, there is no one swing model that is absolute. On the PGA Tour we see slow, smooth passes and swings that would cause severe injury if emulated. We often accept advice and try things that will bring us closer to our goal of breaking 80...90... or simply getting into double figures for the first time. Often we follow the advice without knowing why. Golf is a mysterious game and the why of how we swing is part of golf's most interesting lore.

Why should the left arm remain straight during the swing?

At the moment of impact the left arm must be fully extended in order to let the hands come through in a smooth, powerful motion. During the backswing the left arm remains straight in order to maintain a smooth, wide arc for the swing. If the left elbow breaks down, extra motion is required to bring the clubface back to the intended plane. The result is a loss of power and accuracy.

Why is a slow takeaway important to a good swing?

Sam Snead once compared taking a club back to taking a hammer back to strike a nail. To really drive the nail you draw the hammer back slowly. The same principle holds true in the golf swing. A fast backswing makes it very difficult to control the position at the top of the swing and can throw the clubhead off the intended plane, causing a loop or other movement to get the clubhead back onto the proper path. A slow takeaway promotes a rhythm and tempo that is easier to control and repeat.

Why is it so important to keep your head down during the swing?

It is not so much important to keep your head down as it is to keep it still. The head should be considered the hub of a wheel for your shoulders and arms, creating a center for the arc and plane of the swing. If your head bobs up or down, a top or fat shot can result. If your head moves backward or forward, the plane of the swing can be altered, causing a push or pull with the ball flying left or right of the intended path.

Why are many chips stubbed or hit fat?

The most common cause of a stubbed chip shot is being too wristy. A player who uses his or her hands to direct the force and path of the clubhead takes a strong chance of hitting behind the ball. The best way to avoid this problem is to keep a firm left wrist and use a pendulum-type swing that is made with the arms. Many top players use the reverse overlap putting grip and a putting stroke to create the desired effect. Strike the ball as you would a putt and let the natural loft of the club get the ball into the air.

Why are most putts missed?

Many professionals believe that the main cause of the missed putt is the mishit. A mishit occurs when the ball is struck inside or outside the sweet spot on the putter's face. A second cause is misalignment, in which the putter face is slightly open or slightly closed at the address. Errors in judging the amount of break and the strength required are also key in making a successful putt. Finally, there is the uncontrollable factor of the green itself. Grass texture and tiny bumps may contribute more to missed putts than we generally think. In *The Search for the Perfect Swing*, Alastair Cochran and John Stobbs tell of a putting machine set up to make putts perfect in alignment and speed. At twenty feet the machine could only make 50 percent of its putts because of inconsistencies in the green.

Why do shanks occur?

The shanked shot is one in which the ball strikes the hosel on the inside part of the clubface. The ball shoots out to the right at almost a 90-degree angle from your target line. Generally, the shank is caused by one of two things: 1) taking the club to the inside too quickly and either coming back into the ball at a sharp angle from the inside or looping the club to the outside and cutting back to the ball at an angle; or 2) poor balance in which you move onto your toes at impact. Shanks often occur when the ball lies below your feet.

Cure the shank by being careful during the takeaway, ensuring that the clubface goes straight back from the ball instead of being jerked to the inside. Set your weight on the insides of your feet and keep the head as still as possible during the swing.

Why do hooks run when they land, while fades tend to stop more quickly?

A hooked or drawn shot is generally produced by a closed clubface, a fade or slice by an opened one. An opened face creates more loft and thus a higher shot with more backspin. The closed-face shot tends to fly lower and have less backspin.

Why are touring pros so accurate and weekend players so dismal in hitting wedge shots to the green?

There are several reasons for this pattern. Mainly, the touring pros use a different type of swing for the wedge as opposed to the other clubs. Weekend players tend to take the club back in the one-piece motion and wide arc that is fine for most full shots. The touring pro uses a backswing that is wristy and upright and a sharp descending downswing that pinches the ball out of the turf. The pro also keeps leg movement to a minimum and lets the hands and arms swing the club for greater accuracy.

Why is a grip said to be "weak" or "strong"?

These terms refer to the amount of hand action produced by the placement of the left or leading hand on the club. In a weak grip, the left hand is turned toward the left with the V in the hand pointing toward the left shoulder. A weak grip prevents the right hand from rolling over to close the face of the club and causes a hooked shot. A strong grip is just the opposite: the hands are turned toward the right, allowing a free and powerful hand action that promotes a hook. Most pros advocate a neutral grip that has the Vs pointing to the cheeks.

Why is it that many players fail to improve their swings despite much practice?

Many players confuse hitting balls with practice. If you watch golfers at a crowded driving range you will see many who are hitting ball after ball with the same club (usually a driver) without ever checking their grip, stance or alignment. Every shot in practice should be hit at a target with concentration on the fundamentals and an evaluation of the result.

Why do many top players place their left index finger over the fingers of their right hand when putting?

This putting grip is called the reverse-overlap grip. By placing the left finger over the fingers of the right, the hands tend to work as a one-piece unit. If the hands are spread apart on the shaft, as in a baseball grip, the putting stroke becomes wristy. A wristy stroke is unpredictable and more difficult to control. Most top players try to use a pendulum-type putting stroke in which the swinging action is originated in the larger muscles of the arms and shoulders.

Why do many top players use a waggle or slight movement before they start the backswing?

Basically there are two reasons for the movements that precede the backswing. Firstly, the small movements such as drawing the club back slightly from the ball, serves as a mini-rehearsal for the actual path of the backswing. These movements also serve to break the tension of holding a club stationary. The other slight movements, such as moving the hands forward or bending the right knee forward just prior to the backswing, are often referred to as a "forward press." The forward press is a small movement in the opposite direction of the backswing that helps prevent a jerky motion in starting the club back from a standing position. In earlier days, the forward press was much more pronounced; the modern swing has greatly reduced this movement to only a slight move, which breaks inertia just before the club is drawn back.

Why is it common to hit "fliers," shots that sail with little backspin on them, from the rough?

In heavy rough the grass directly behind the ball becomes trapped between the ball and clubface at impact. The grass prevents the grooves of the clubface from grabbing the ball, so it tends to fly like a knuckleball through the air. It is best to take one less club and use a sharp descending downswing to snap the ball out with a minimum of interference from the grass. The ball will run farther, compensating for the change.

Why have so many golfers bought golf instructional videos?

It is estimated that 90 percent of all American homes will have VCRs in the near future. This technology is well suited for golf instruction for several reasons. Because of the tremendous impact of television, Americans are increasingly becoming visual learners: they absorb and retain video material more readily than what they read or hear. Psychologists have discovered that many people are able to copy a particular athletic movement after watching filmed demonstrations. Golf videos enable many golfers to study the golf swings of the greats up close; they can emulate these swings in practice. Many golfers have found that watching videos just prior to playing helps with tempo and implants an overall swingthought for the proper golf swing.

Why do golfers look at the ball rather than the hole when putting?

In almost every other sport that requires accuracy in propelling a missile (throwing a baseball, football, horseshoes, bowling, basketball, etc.), a player looks at the target rather than the ball or object being thrown or propelled. The main difference between these sports and golf is that a golf ball is being moved from a still position that is not in contact with any part of the player's body or equipment before the propelling action. When putting, the head must remain still so the body will not push or pull the ball off line. Many players have tried looking at the hole instead of the cup and report very good results for a short time. Johnny Miller putted by looking at the hole for a season or two on the Tour. The technique seems to work for a short time because the golfer has to increase his concentration with the new technique, and looking at the hole helps keep the head still. It tends to fade in effectiveness over time, as the concentration level wanes and the player becomes comfortable with the technique.

Why is the downhill-sidehill shot so difficult?

There are two main reasons why this is a difficult shot for the average golfer: 1) gravity and 2) lack of practice. The golf swing requires proper balance and a shifting of weight from the back to the front foot on the downswing. By setting up on a downhill-sidehill lie, you are pulled by gravity in a way that seriously affects your balance and swing plane. The key to overcoming this situation is to reverse the effects of gravity. By bending your knees more, standing more upright and keeping your weight on the back foot as you set up, you are creating a stance that compensates for gravity. The second cause of difficulty for the average golfer is lack of practice in this situation. These tough lies are not as much fun to practice as hitting drives off a tee, so most golfers avoid them. The best advice is to find a spot that simulates a severe downhill-sidehill situation and hit balls until you gain confidence and a good sense of technique and feel for the shot.

Why is it important to keep your head over the ball while putting?

Keeping your head over the ball gets your eyes over the ball and along the target line. In doing this, you can move the putter back and forth along the target line and strike the ball along the intended path. If your head is back from the target line, you get a distorted view of how the putter is swung back and through.

Why does wind cause so many problems for the average golfer?

As a golf ball only weighs 1.62 ounces the wind can play a significant role in the flight of a golf shot. Because the wind can affect a ball greatly, many golfers change their swings and tactics to a point where they become self-defeating. Generally, a golfer is better off swinging more slowly in the wind rather than speeding up. Teeing the ball low can cause a lower flight, but many times it only makes the tee shot more difficult to hit. Tee the ball only slightly lower than normal and concentrate on good contact. In club selection, the rule of thumb is to take one more club than is normally needed for every ten miles-per-hour of wind against and one club less for every ten miles-per-hour of wind behind you.

Why are the long irons so difficult to hit?

There are several reasons why the long irons present problems. First, they have long shafts and little loft. These clubs require a long, full backswing and a smooth, sweeping motion down and through the ball. Most high handicappers run into problems with the long irons because they swing too hard in an attempt to gain distance, disrupting the swing plane. The long irons will provide distance if struck solidly with a smooth swing.

Why do some golfers tee the ball high, then tilt the tee and ball backward as far as possible?

The idea behind this maneuver is to create lift. The driver has a very shallow face (about 10 degrees of loft) and is meant to strike the ball on a slightly upward swing path. Teeing the ball on a slight slant gives the impression of hitting at a ball that is set to lift off. While the effect of this type of tee is probably psychological at best, many players feel it is a helpful technique.

Why is it that many players hit great shots at a driving range but cannot bring the same shots to the golf course?

There are two possible explanations for this common complaint: tension and self-correction. At the driving range, the golfer is relatively free of tension. Tension restricts the swing and speeds up tempo. On the golf course with your Sunday foursome, tension is present in every shot whether or not you are aware of it. Secondly, at a driving range you might hit ten 5-irons in a row. As you hit each one you make subtle corrections and gain a feel for the shot. On the golf course, you might hit two 5-irons all day—both in isolated instances under pressure. The key is to develop muscle memory, reduce tension and trust your swing.

Why are trap shots so difficult?

Actually, the trap shot is not too difficult for players who know how to execute it. Most golfers do not practice this shot and use the wrong technique to get the ball out of a trap. Too often, the average golfer tries to scoop the ball out by using a wide arc and extra motion at impact to lift the ball up and out. The proper method is to make a slow smooth backswing that is very upright and a sharp descending downswing that cuts into the sand about two inches behind the ball. The club should pass under the ball and the swing should be completed with a high finish.

Why is one of golf's most common faults called a "reverse pivot" and what exactly is it?

The reverse pivot comes from shifting weight to the back foot during the downswing. In the proper golf swing, the hips should slide forward at the top of the swing and the weight should shift to the front foot. In the reverse pivot a player shifts to the back foot in an attempt to get more power or to scoop the ball into the air. The reverse pivot usually produces topped shots that dribble along the ground. Many golfers who played baseball as youngsters have a tendency to shift to the back foot as is taught in the baseball swing. But the power of a golf swing comes from centrifugal force; the power of a baseball swing comes from the arms and hands.

Why is it that many top golfers seldom take practice swings, but take several when making a wedge shot?

Many top players do not take full practice swings because they have honed their swings through practice and know exactly how the full swing feels. By eliminating practice swings they conserve energy. However, when faced with a short pitch or chip, many top players do take rehearsal swings. Distance on short shots is determined and regulated by the length of the backswing. The good players take a series of swings until they find the length of the backswing required for the upcoming shot. With the proper amount of backswing in their muscle memory they now have a good sense of the shot.

Why is it that most beginners start out slicing instead of hooking?

There are two main reasons for this pattern: grip and swing plane. Most people who grip a golf club for the first time hold it so that the left hand is turned to the right, a very natural way to hold a club and the preferred method for gripping a baseball bat. However, in golf the wrists turn or pronate and do not break as in baseball. The incorrect grip leaves the face of the club open, and the ball flies off with sidespin. The beginner also has a tendency to hit the ball from the outside, which produces a sidespin as well. The inside-out swing plane seems counterproductive to the raw beginner, who is slicing the ball to the right anyway.

Why is shoulder-turn so important to a good swing?

Full shoulder-turn during the swing creates a wider arc. The wider the arc, the longer the clubhead will travel and thus build up speed. Clubhead speed, of course, translates into distance, but a good shoulder-turn may also help accuracy. In returning the clubhead to the ball it is easier to control the large muscle groups involved in a turn than it is to control the wrists and hands. The good player allows the big muscle groups to control and drive the swing and the hands and arms to transmit the power.

Why is it difficult to judge distances on desert courses?

In general, desert courses have few trees and are very flat from tee to green. Without these terrain features, gaining a perspective is difficult. As you look at a distant point, your mind and eye compute distance by the relative size of objects near that point. Telephone poles along a highway, for example, help us determine distance by the apparent size. Many top players use their knowledge of distance to their advantage by visualizing how far they can hit a 9-iron, then how far for an 8 and so on until they gauge the right club to cover the distance to the pin rather than relying on estimation.

Why do most amateurs strike behind or hit a "fat" shot on a downhill lie?

The most common reason for a fat shot on a downhill lie is the player's subconscious thought of getting the ball up into the air. The main culprit is dipping the right or back knee at impact in a futile effort to get under the ball. The cure is to keep the knees flexed and level to the lie as much as possible by swinging with the upper body and striking the ball with a sharp, descending blow.

Why do golfers take a backswing?

The backswing helps the golfer coil—the body, back in a smooth manner, helps set the club in a position to return to the ball. If one started from the top without a backswing, it would be difficult to get in the correct position each time. It would take exceptional skill to return the clubhead accurately to the ball. It is the same principle as a carpenter swinging his hammer back to drive a nail.

Why is grip pressure a key ingredient to a good golf swing?

Most amateurs grip the club too tightly. A pro can tell what kind of golfer a player is just by looking at his/her grip. If a player holds the club so that the muscles of the forearm are tight, then the grip is too firm. A light grip allows for the proper cocking of the wrists on the backswing and the release of the hands at maximum speed through impact. Tight muscles are slow muscles and loose muscle are quick muscles.

Why do tour pros hit the ball so far while looking as if they are swinging effortlessly?

In one word—torque. A good player will turn his/her shoulders back to 90 degrees or more while only turning the hips about one fifth of that distance on the backswing. This move creates tension or torque between the upper and lower body that is much like a spring being wound then uncoiled. This coiled position is often referred to as the "X Factor" or "creating the gap" by the pros.

Why do good players make a slight movement before starting the club back?

Almost every good player makes a slight movement called "forward press" before starting the club back. The forward press breaks inertia, and prevents starting the club back with a jerky motion. Some players make a slight forward movement with their hands; others use a little flex move in their knees. Jack Nicklaus is famous for turning his head slightly to the right before he brings the club back.

The Professionals

In the 1920s country clubs began to spread across the country. In the winter months, the club pros headed to Florida and, naturally, competitions sprang up. Gradually, these competitions spread into Georgia and the Carolinas as the pros headed north in the spring. In this way the beginnings of the Tour were formed. While famous amateurs Francis Ouimet and Bobby Jones had dominated the golfing public's attention for years, new names such as Sarazen, Hagen, Hogan, Nelson and Snead swept across the nation in the thirties, forties and fifties. The charisma of Arnold Palmer and televised tournaments brought the general public to the game and set the foundation for the tremendous boom in the game today.

The PGA and LPGA Tours are followed by hundreds of thousands of fans with deep interest and dedication. They watch in quiet flocks called galleries, carry no banners, applaud all competitors and never pull against anyone. The golf gallery empathizes with the competitors in a way that is seldom matched in any other sport. Most of us will never know what it is like to look at a Roger Clemens fastball or to trap-block Howie Long. Yet each member of the gallery knows exactly what it feels like to have a five-foot downhill curler for a needed par.

The pros are the epitome of mastery. We copy their mannerisms, use their equipment, wear their clothes and try to swing their swings. The glamour and mastery of the professionals offer more than just heroes to emulate, they represent the state of the art for millions of would-be artists.

Why don't players on the professional tour concede holes or putts in sudden-death playoffs when the hole is obviously lost?

Most of the PGA tournaments are medal play and require that all holes be completed. If a tournament goes into a playoff, it does not automatically become a match-play event.

Why did tournaments stop paying appearance fees to the top pros?

The PGA outlawed the practice of paying appearance fees because several agencies gained too much power by having many big-name players in their stables. Such an agency could make or break a tournament just by the number of big names that they could promise or withhold. The PGA prohibited the practice in order to bring stability for tournament committees, television and the fans.

Why do touring pros have such large bags?

Besides being moving billboards for golf equipment manufacturers, the golf bags must carry many items to meet contingencies. A typical staff bag might carry the following: twenty-four golf balls, tees, six gloves (pros change them about every six holes), a sweater, a rainsuit, a rain hood to protect the clubs, an extra pair of golf shoes and socks (in case of wet or very humid weather), an extra towel, an umbrella, spikes and a spike wrench, a yardage book, a rules book, coins, sunscreen, Band-aids, pencils and fruit (for snacks).

Why do touring pros sometimes look into the cup while sizing up a putt?

They are not looking into the cup but at the rim around it. If the grass is clipped very closely on one side of the cup it may indicate that a putt will break in the opposite direction. As the mower passed over the cup it clipped the grass on the higher part more closely. Also, they inspect the rim to see if it has become broken or worn. If the rim is worn they may have to hit a putt that "dies" at the hole rather than a firm putt that might spin out.

Why do many pros carry three wedges in their bags?

The third wedge added to the pitching and sand wedges is a club with an extremely high degree of loft, ranging up to about 65 degrees. This wedge is used for finesse shots of under 50 yards where the pro needs to pop the ball over a bunker or water and make it stop quickly. The club comes in handy as well for shots over trees, off hard pan and on steep downhill lies near the green. Many pros take the 3-iron out of the bag to make room for the third wedge.

Why do touring pros tend to walk by themselves in tournaments and not talk much with fellow competitors or the gallery during a round?

It is not because they are unfriendly. The pros need to concentrate on the strategy required for the upcoming shot and do not want to become distracted. Secondly, under the Rules of Golf, they may not receive advice or assistance from anyone except their caddies. Should they accidentally discuss such things as club selection or course condition they may face a penalty. There are also penalties for slow play that each player must be aware of as he or she plays a round.

Why do touring pros sometimes look straight up when they are selecting a club?

Some may be praying. Most likely, however, the pros are looking at the tops of the trees. The winds at the tree-top level will have a far more pronounced effect on their shots than the wind at ground level.

Why are purses so large today compared to a relatively short time ago?

At one time golf was considered to be the pastime of the rich. Since World War II the middle class has taken to golf in a continuous period of growth. Professional golf moved into the period of big paydays in the 1960s, when television began to tap into the growing interest in the game. At that time, the charismatic Arnold Palmer was the reigning king of golf whose good looks and daring play brought thousands of spectators to tournaments and sponsors to television. With Jack Nicklaus's brilliant play, Lee Trevino's color and Gary Player's power, personalities soon emerged as drawing cards. Corporate sponsors are well aware that the golfing fan is a good consumer and thus have been eager to have their names associated with golf's elite. While golf's ratings may be lower than other sporting events on television, the golf viewer is a prized consumer, as evidenced by the types of products advertised and the amount of money put out to attract the big names in golf.

Why do touring pros have to keep their own score?

The nature of the game demands that the "honor system" be used. In golf, the player himself may frequently be the only one aware of a rules infraction. For example, a player may be the only one to see any of the following infractions: a ball moves slightly after address; a new ball is put into play; a club is grounded slightly in a hazard; or a ball is struck twice during a swing. Most pros hold the integrity of the game in high regard and will call penalties on themselves without hesitation.

Why don't touring pros pick their own balls out of the cup after making a long putt?

To avoid creating additional spike marks near the hole, the pros have their caddies, who usually wear sneakers, retrieve the ball from the hole.

Why is the PGA Tour considered one of the most difficult major league sports to enter?

To qualify for a spot on the PGA golfers must play well over a period of elimination rounds against the best players in the world. The players on tour who finish between 1 and 125 on the annual money list are exempt from qualifying. Players who finish 126 to 150 must qualify at a 108-hole tournament in December. For players seeking to break into the Tour, qualification begins in early fall with a 72-hole tournament followed by a second elimination tournament of 72 holes. The initial field of 1,750 is cut down to 155 players who join the twenty-five touring pros for the December tournament to select the fifty players who will receive tour cards for the coming year. The 108-hole tournament is a pressure-packed event where a bad hole might mean a year's plans down the drain.

Why do touring pros change balls every few holes?

Golf balls tend to get out of round after being hit several times. The pros change balls to prevent having to putt with a ball that is out of round and would not roll in a true manner.

When sizing up a putt, why do touring pros look at the edge of the green, even if their ball is nowhere near it?

The pros often look for places where water has run off the green. The flow of water from a green may assist them in judging slopes and breaks otherwise indiscernible.

Why do pros on the tour often practice after their round?

Many pros say they practice after a round for two reasons—they played well or they played poorly. If they have played very well they like to keep hitting balls in order to keep the good tempo and rhythm going and get it into their muscle memory. On the other hand, if they have been having trouble with a particular part of their game, say driving, they will hit balls until they feel that they have worked out the problem and their confidence has returned.

Why do touring pros dread wet conditions the most?

The pros do not like wet conditions because reaction of the ball is unpredictable. The grooves on the irons become filled with water and reduce spin on the ball, which causes a knuckleball effect called a "flyer." This effect has the pros guessing at how far the ball will fly and how it will react upon hitting the green.

Why do touring pros write something on their golf balls before playing?

The pros are marking their balls for identification purposes. Because many pros use the same brand of golf balls, they place a few dots or circles on the ball to guard against mix-ups.

Why do touring pros count their clubs on the first tee?

The Rules of Golf allow only fourteen clubs during play. The pros often swap clubs and try new clubs on the practice tee as they warm up for a round, and it is not uncommon for a stray club to wind up in a pro's bag accidentally.

Why did the PGA Championship change from match to stroke play?

In a word, television. A match play event is very difficult to follow in a television format, with some seventy-two pairings on the first day and the chance that the stars will not be available for action at air time. In a round-robin system, players are eliminated until there are only two left for the championship round. The championship takes place on Sunday afternoon, and the cameras have to follow only two players for over four hours. The PGA decided that in order to accommodate the television audience, a stroke event would be more entertaining and profitable.

Why do the touring pros work their feet so deeply into the sand when they are in a bunker?

There are three reasons for this maneuver: by sinking their feet into the sand they anchor themselves and prevent slipping while taking a swing; they lower their bodies so the club will enter the sand behind the ball; and they are able to test the consistency of the sand under the Rules of Golf.

Why do the touring pros sometimes walk up to the flagstick, pull it out and then put it back in before making a chip shot?

They want to ascertain if the pin is leaning in any direction. Sometimes a caddy will not place it all the way into the liner hole in the cup. When this happens the pin may lean against the player's line and keep a ball from dropping. The player may also be testing the rigidity of the pin. If the pin is very rigid, and the chip is makeable, the pro will probably remove the pin.

Why is Al Geiberger called "Mr. 59"?

Al Geiberger has won ten PGA Tour events including the 1966 PGA Championship, but he will forever be known for shooting the lowest score in a PGA event to date, a 59 in the second round of the Danny Thomas Memphis Classic in 1977. Geiberger's business card opens to a replica of the Colonial Club's scoreboard and the hole-by-hole tally of his OUT 29-IN 30-59.

Why do many touring pros stand directly behind the ball before taking their address?

The pros are sighting down the target line by lining up the ball with the spot where they want it to land. Many pick an intermediate target as well, a leaf, divot or discolored patch of grass a few feet in front of the ball and along the target line. When they take the address position they line up their feet, hips and shoulders along the line created by the ball and the intermediate target a few feet away.

Why don't the touring pros use yellow or orange balls?

The colored balls are primarily intended for those golfers who have difficulty finding their balls. The touring pros have little problem with lost balls. Additionally, the pros have spent a lifetime practicing with white golf balls, and many find the change to bright colors distracting.

Why do many PGA tournaments feature Pro-Am tournaments as a prelude to the actual event?

Money—the Pro-Am tournaments make up a large percentage of the prize money offered at each tournament. Entry fees for an amateur in these tournaments easily run into the $3,000-$5,000 range. Multiply that entry fee by 300 to 400 amateurs and the value of such events can be readily appreciated. Many corporations use the Pro-Ams as perks for deserving executives and enticements for prospective customers. There are long waiting lists for the chance to play in some of the more prestigious tourneys such as the Bob Hope Desert Classic or the Dinah Shore. The invitation list to some of these events reads like a *Who's Who* of the rich and famous.

Why do touring pros always finish their preround practice by hitting some soft wedge shots?

The pros like to finish their warm-up practice by hitting soft wedge shots because the practice promotes "feel" and develops the smooth rhythm that they want to bring to the first tee.

Why are the pros on the bottom of a tournament scoreboard called the "dawn patrol"?

The pairings for a tournament are done by score, with the leaders teeing off last on the final two days of the tournament. Thus, players at the bottom, or those who just made the cut, must tee off very early in the morning.

Why is it said that "you drive for show but putt for dough"?

It is felt that good putting is more important to winning money on the Tour. Statistics generally support this axiom. In 1987 Curtis Strange, the Tour's leading money-winner with $925,941, was 107th in driving distance (260.6 yards) but sixteenth in putting with 1.77 putts per hole. Ben Crenshaw ($638,194) was eighty-sixth in driving but first in putting. The Tour's long-drive champion for a year has never won a tournament in the year that he held the distinction since Tour records have been kept.

Why are cameras banned at many Tour events?

The pros are used to most normal crowd noises, but the anticipation of a camera click is very disconcerting to the players during actual play.

Why are the pros surveyed just before teeing off on the first and last days of a tournament?

The surveys are conducted by several independent market research companies who sell their information to the golf industry. Golf ball manufacturers, for example, use this information in their advertisements. Market research has shown that the golfing public, very conscious of the equipment and clothing used by the top professionals, make purchases (over a billion dollars a year) according to what is hot on the Tour. As an example, when Jack Nicklaus won the 1986 Masters using an oversized putter, McGregor was immediately overwhelmed with orders for it.

Why do touring pros mark their ball and lift it when it is a very simple putt?

They mark it to clean it of any grass or sand that may have clung to the ball on the prior putt. In addition, they also check to see if the ball is resting in a spike mark or ball divot, which might affect the roll of the ball after impact. This procedure may seem tedious to the average golfer, but the amount of money involved is considerable and the pros do not want to leave anything to chance.

Why do touring pros have brand names displayed on everything possible?

Touring pros receive all of their equipment and clothes free from the manufacturers. In addition, they receive cash bonuses for appearing on television, finishing high, or winning a tournament. Pros receive lucrative bonuses from golf ball companies, club makers and clothing manufacturers for a win that can earn them tens of thousands of dollars.

Why don't the men pros wear shorts on very hot days?

The PGA Tour has strict guidelines for everything from abusive language to appearance. In the appearance category shorts are forbidden. It is felt that full-length golf pants are more in keeping with the Tour's image of gentlemen playing a gentleman's game.

Why must an aspiring touring pro provide his financial statement to the PGA Tour before he is eligible to play?

The PGA wants to ensure that the pro has the financial ability to stay on the tour for the year. Traveling expenses, entrance fees, caddies and living expenses may run over $50,000 a year following the sun on the PGA tour. The PGA officials do not want no-shows or open slots at a tournament because a pro could not afford the trip.

Why is the LPGA's Hall of Fame considered to be one of the toughest in all of sport?

The LPGA Hall of Fame has exacting criteria for admittance compared to the election format used in other sports. To be admitted to the LPGA Hall of Fame, a woman has to win thirty victories on the tour, including two different majors; thirty-five victories with one major; or forty victories without a win in a major.

Why do some touring pros have their caddies read their putts?

Most touring pros read their putts alone. Some have their caddies give their opinions on the speed and break, and others use their caddies as sounding boards, explaining the putt as they think out loud.

Why do pros on the Senior Tour wear a clip on their belts?

The money clip that the seniors wear has the Senior Tour logo on it and serves as identification that the player is eligible to play in Senior Tour events.

Why do pros hold their putters in front of their eyes when lining up a putt? Just what are they looking for?

This technique is called "plumb-bobbing." The purpose of plumbing is to help determine slope. By holding the putter perpendicular to the hole, the player can see if the cup is tilted, a clear indication of slope.

Why do many pros insist that their caddies carry the golf balls in their pockets?

This practice is called "warming the eggs." Many pros believe that warming the golf balls help them to fly farther. While warming does enhance the elasticity of the ball, it would require illegal means to raise the temperature of the ball to get any significant benefits from it.

Why do many pros stare at their coin before they put it down to mark their ball on the green?

Most of the time it is superstition. Many pros have quirks in marking a ball on the green with a coin in a certain manner. Some always place the coin heads up with the face looking at the hole. Others are making sure that they are using their lucky coin. If they have to move their mark for another player, many will flip the coin to remind themselves to move it back to the original spot before they putt.

Why is it more difficult to make the LPGA Tour than the men's PGA Tour?

Women can only qualify for the LPGA Tour through the 72-hole qualification school. Men can gain entry to their tour by either the qualification school or by finishing in the top 15 on the Nike Tour. While the women have a minor league type tour called "The Futures," winning on that tour or placing high on the money list does not gain entry to the LPGA.

Why do the Tour Professionals practice after a great round?

Many tour players will practice after having a great round simply to keep "in the zone." In other words, when they find themselves hitting the ball perfectly, they feel that by continuing to hit balls while they have that feeling, tempo and rhythm, it will help them capture their swing patterns.

Why do some professionals take a semi-back-swing just before they make their actual swing?

Players such as Justin Leonard and Tiger Woods often take a semi-backswing just prior to the actual swing to rehearse the swing plane of their backswing. This little move helps them to take the club back in a path that is not too inside or too outside of their intended backswing. The waggle lets them feel the proper takeaway path.

Why do some caddies tip the pin backward while tending it for their player on tour?

Caddies often tip the pin backward from the hole because it gives the player a sense of the line to the hole. With the pin tilted backward, it looks like a line being extended beyond the hole to the player.

Why are some professionals chipping with fairway woods?

Several professionals have begun chipping with fairway woods under certain conditions. If the ball is on a thin lie, having little grass underneath it, or on a course rough around the green, then the pros may use the fairway wood. It avoids the chance of hitting behind the ball, or fat. The wood tends to glide on the ground, gets the ball moving with a slight bump into the air, and then rolls onto the ground.

Why do professionals always seem not to know the Rules and ask for a rules official when they have a question?

It is not that they do not know the Rules of Golf as much as it is avoiding the possibility of being disqualified, or getting a better interpretation than they might get from a fellow competitor. For example, if a player has to take a drop and if for some reason his drop is not within the Rules, knowingly or unknowingly, a fellow competitor or official who witnessed it may question it after the round. Then, he/she may be disqualified and ineligible to win any money. By having a rules official present, the player gets a stamp of approval right on the spot.

A fellow competitor has an obligation to "protect the field." The competitor will make judgements on rulings that makes sure that the player is conforming to the Rules and not taking any advantage. A pro might get a better break from a rules official. A fellow competitor might be more conservative in granting relief or assisting in interpreting a Rule.

Why don't professionals take a practice putt after they hole during a tournament as they do in the Ryder Cup matches?

The Rules of Golf prohibit practicing on the course during medal or stroke play. Thus, taking a putt over after finishing a hole would be a two stroke penalty. In match play, such as in the Ryder Cup, "practice" on the course is allowed under the Rules. In this format, players often re-play a putt to get the feel of a green or see why they missed a putt after they have holed out.

The Course

One of golf's unique features is that no two playing fields in the world are alike. Subtle changes brought about by wind, rain, sun or the growth of grass can have pronounced effects on the game. Golf's architects have continually blended nature and the spirit of the game to create character and challenge in the holes that they have built.

From St. Andrews to the stadium courses of today, the golf course has served as a test of strategy and skill that is seldom found in any other arena. The playing fields themselves—Muirfield, Troon, Baltusrol, the Country Club—have earned sacred spots in golf lore and legend. The courses are sources of controversy and debate, love and respect, fear and dread. Golfers relive courses as soldiers relive battlefields. Certain holes live in fame and infamy for the deeds performed on them. Though the course is the opponent, it must be the most loved opponent in the annals of sport.

Why is it said that "putts always break toward the water"?

It is not that the water has some magnetic force on the ball. Water, of course, seeks its lowest level, which is usually a body of water—an ocean, lake or pond near the green. As water drains toward the body of water it tends to shape the slope toward the direction of the pond or lake. Additionally, the grain on the green tends to grow in the direction of a water source. These factors cause a putt to break in the direction of a body of water.

Why is "The Country Club" of Brookline so named?

The site of the 1988 U.S. Open has been referred to as The Country Club since its beginning. It was built as a "park where members may be free from the annoyances of horse railroads and meet for pleasure, driving and riding." The club was formally established in 1882. The Country Club gained fame when a young Francis Ouimet won the 1913 U.S. Open in a playoff against Harry Vardon and Ted Ray.

Why do many golf courses in Japan have two greens per hole?

The Japanese climate has extreme ranges in temperature. Bent grass, the preferred grass for greens, tends to burn out quickly in the hot, humid summers. To solve this problem, the Japanese decided to build two greens per hole. One green would have bent grass, which would be regrown each year. The other green would be of *korai,* a very tough grass imported from Korea which can withstand harsh winters. Thus, Japanese clubs offer their members two greens, one for summer and one for winter.

Why is the famous Olympic Course in San Francisco called "the course that was built in reverse"?

In 1922 the Olympic Club, a private social club, purchased a course near Lake Merced called Lakeside. The course was located on the bare side of a large hill that ran down to the lake. The Olympic Club immediately began planting eucalyptus, pine and cypress trees to outline each of the eighteen holes. The trees matured some twenty-five years later to become an essential part of the challenge and beauty of Olympic. That trees were planted on an existing course rather than having holes carved out from a forest gave birth to the expression "built in reverse."

Why are there "dogleg" holes?

Dogleg holes were first designed about seventy years ago to break the monotony of straightaway holes and afford the golf architect some leeway in matching design characteristics and golfing skills. The dogleg hole may tempt the long hitter to cut over trees or water to gain a closer approach shot. Additionally, bunkers, rough, water and trees can be strategically placed on a dogleg to reward the great shot and punish the stray one as few straight holes could.

Why are there so many tee locations and so much teeing space at most courses?

The amount and location of teeing ground determine the leeway architect and greenskeeper have when planning shotmaking and maintenance. Nine-hole courses often have significant differences in the tee-markers from front to back nine to bring variety and afford players the challenge of hitting different shots on the same hole. In championship conditions, the tee locations may be used to add distance and increase the level of difficulty of a hole. To set a course record, a competitor must use the back tees.

Why are flagsticks all the same height?

The USGA recommends that the flagstick be a minimum of seven feet high. Manufacturers generally adhere to this size because of perspective. If flagsticks varied in height from course to course it would be difficult to judge distance.

Why is the stretch between the eleventh and thirteenth holes at Augusta National called "Amen Corner"?

The origin of the term "Amen Corner" is credited to Herbert Warren Wind who noted that if you can negotiate these three holes in par a prayer is in order. The three holes have had a long history in deciding the Masters. The eleventh is 445 yards, with water to the left and behind the green. The second shot is usually a 4- to 6-iron that must be strategically placed. The twelfth is a par 3 of only 155 yards, but wind conditions and pin placement make this one of the most difficult holes on the course. The thirteenth is a 485-yard dogleg par 5. Water runs the entire left side and crosses in front of the green. The water and traps surrounding the green give pause to the long hitters who try to hit this green in two.

Why are the tees that are farthest back called "tiger tees"?

Very good golfers were once commonly referred to as tigers, poor ones as rabbits. The very good players would naturally play from the back tees.

Why is one trap at Oakmont called "Church Pews"?

Between the third and fourth holes at Oakmont there is a trap that is 60 yards long that is set to catch stray drives from both holes. The trap has seven grassy ridges that run across it giving the appearance of church pews.

Why is the fourth hole at Baltusrol famous in golfing lore?

Baltusrol hired the famous golf architect Robert Trent Jones to toughen up the course for the 1954 U.S. Open. After he finished his task by making alterations on several holes, the members complained that he had made the course too tough. The new fourth hole, for example, required a tee shot of almost 200 yards across water to a well-bunkered par 3. Jones, along with the club pro, club president and the chairman of the Open committee, actually played the fourth hole to rate its toughness for themselves. After the first three had hit their shots, Jones teed up and holed out the shot for an ace. He simply shrugged: "As you can see, gentlemen, this hole is not too tough."

Why is Pine Valley often considered the top golf course in the United States?

Pine Valley, located in Clementon, New Jersey, places a premium on accuracy and distance that few courses can match. Many of the holes at Pine Valley do not have continuous fairways but rather narrow and demanding landing areas. Stray shots do not land in simple rough: sandy scrub brush and water abound along the landing areas. The par 3s demand that the ball land and hold the green, and the par 5s average around 600 yards and require three perfect golf shots to get home.

Why is the eighteenth tee at Harbour Town called "Nicklaus tee"?

Harbour Town Golf Links, located on Hilton Head Island in South Carolina, is the site of the Heritage Golf Classic. The eighteenth hole has several tees, but one is located in a position that requires a drive of 250 yards to a peninsula portion of the fairway. This tee is not used too often in tournament play because of its extreme difficulty. Many Harbour Town members say it would take one of Jack's drives just to reach the fairway.

Why do greenskeepers use the term "put to bed" in regard to a golf course?

Greenskeepers in the north "put the course to bed" in late fall. The procedure usually entails covering the greens to prevent damage from frost and ice, placing snow fences around greens and tees to prevent skiers or snowmobiles from cutting tracks into the turf, and digging special drainage ditches for traps or particularly wet spots along the course. The purpose, of course, is to survive the winter in good shape and be ready for an early opening in the spring.

Why is the sand trap on the seventh hole at Pine Valley called "Hell's Half-acre"?

The seventh hole at Pine Valley has been called the most exacting par 5 in the world. Its 585-yard length is not the real problem: the huge expanse of sand and scrub brush that begins 285 yards off the tee and extends for over 100 yards creates one of the most challenging holes in the game. In order to play this hole in par, you have to hit a grassy landing area on the second shot that is 385 yards from the tee. In other words, it takes two very long and accurate golf shots just to be in position to hit the green with the third. The giant sand trap that defines this golf hole is in the *Guinness Book of World Records* as the world's largest sand trap and is affectionately known as "Hell's Half-acre."

Why is the famous golf course Baltusrol so named?

Located in Springfield, New Jersey, Baltusrol's name is derived from a farmer of Dutch origin named Baltus Roll, who once owned the land.

Why are some courses characterized as "championship"?

A championship course is one that presents situations that a championship caliber player must be able to execute. It should require both distance and accuracy and it should force strategic moves on the part of the competitor. It should also place a degree of difficulty on the finesse shots and reward consistent putting.

Why are those new, very short courses called "Cayman" courses?

Cayman courses, which run around 4,000 yards in length, were first put into use in the Cayman Islands. Special balls that travel a shorter distance than normal are used to play these courses. Cayman courses rose out of the shortage of land tracts required for a full-length course and the steady growth in the number of golfers each year. The first Cayman courses were developed in the early 1980s.

Why does the ball seem to sit up better on the fairways of Florida courses?

Most of the courses in Florida use Bermuda grass, a wiry, coarse-bladed grass that grows well in warm climates. Because Bermuda grass is so thick, it holds the ball up on the fairway much more effectively than grasses such as Poa annua or bent.

Why is the sixteenth hole at Firestone called "The Monster"?

The sixteenth at Firestone is a 625-yard par 5. While downhill, the advantage of the slope is negated by the lie usually left for the long second shot home. Water guards the green in front, prohibiting even the boldest player from firing at the green from a distant, downhill lie. Legend has it that only two players have ever hit the green in two in competition—Firestone's club pro and former PGA Champion Bobby Nichols and Arnold Palmer who used the word "monster" to describe the hole after he took a triple-bogey 8 on it in the 1960 PGA Championship.

When holes are rated for strokes, why are some difficult holes rated lower than holes that seem easier?

Difficulty is not necessarily the main criterion in deciding which holes are to be considered the stroke holes in an order from one to eighteen. The USGA's guidelines call for consideration to be given to a poorer player in a match against a superior player, so that the main criterion is the place where the player needs the stroke the most. Also, the stroke holes are distributed equally on the front and back nines (odd-numbered on the front, even-numbered stroke holes on the back). Though the holes on one nine may be tougher than on the other, the stroke holes still must be distributed equally. Generally holes are graded in the following order: difficult par 5s, difficult par 4s, remaining par 5s, remaining par 4s and par 3s. Of course, exceptions may be made for especially tough par 3s and 4s.

Why is Oakmont famous for its sand traps?

Oakmont opened in 1904 with an incredible 350 bunkers, almost twenty per hole. In order to cut maintenance costs the number was gradually cut to 171.

Why are some courses called "stadium" courses?

Stadium courses are specifically designed to accommodate large galleries for PGA Tour events. Many of the older courses on the tour are surrounded by trees or water that prohibit galleries from getting a good view of the golf action. Stadium courses are designed with large slopes around the greens, viewing perches, walking paths and other facilities to facilitate large groups of golf fans and offer them a better view of play.

Why do some courses have wicker baskets instead of flags on their flagsticks?

Originally flagsticks were just plain staffs. Eventually they sported small disks with the number of the hole on them. Most flagsticks at the turn of the century were about three feet tall. The Sunningdale Course in England used wicker baskets to help golfers see the pin placement better from any angle. The wicker-basket pins were also very popular in England because they did not aid the golfer in determining the strength and direction of the wind. Hugh Wilson designed Merion Golf Club near Philadelphia in 1912. Wilson studied course architecture in England and was impressed with the British tradition. He thought the addition of wicker baskets at Merion would help establish it as a unique course in the United States. Some courses have copied Merion's flagsticks, but the wicker-basket pins are relatively scarce because of cost and maintenance.

Why are some courses called "executive" courses?

Because executive courses are shorter than championship courses, they can be played more quickly, and the busy executive can get a round into his schedule. But the main reason for the rise in the executive course is the scarcity of good golf-course land and the great increase in people playing golf.

Why is Wack-Wack, a course on the Asian Tour, so named?

Often the site of the Philippines Open, Wack-Wack Golf and Country Club is located near Manila. It got its name from the sound of crows, which were extremely numerous and bothersome to the players in the early days of the course.

Why is the famous Golden Horseshoe course in Old Williamstown, Virginia, so named?

In 1716, the governor of Virginia, Alexander Spotswood, led an expedition from Williamsburg over the Appalachians and back. Upon returning to Williamsburg, he gave each member of the expedition a golden horseshoe.

Why is the 10th hole at Carnoustie in Scotland called "South America"?

Legend has it that near the turn of the century a young, local player who had hopes of making his fortune in South America as a golf pro, played a farewell round at Carnoustie. Having celebrated with Scotch before and during the round, he passed out on the 10th hole. The Scots said that is as far as he got.

Why is it that such professionals as Jack Nicklaus, Fuzzy Zoeller and Lloyd Mangrum have called the short par three 12th hole at Augusta National "the hardest hole in golf"?

While the 12th hole at Augusta is only 155 yards long, there are many devilish subtleties about this hole that can drive the very best players to despair. The lightning fast green is only 35 yards wide at some points, there are three bunkers guarding it—two in back and one in front. From the back bunkers, you are faced with a downhill sand shot to a lightning fast green and a severe slope that runs directly into Rae's Creek.

Many players have hit great shots at the pin when it is cut close to the front only to have the ball take a little hop, pick up backspin and roll down the sharp slope to the water.

In addition, the tall pines that surround the hole cause the wind to swirl in various directions, leaving the play at the whim of a sudden gust.

Why did Augusta National ban Gary McCord from telecasting at the Masters?

During a television broadcast of the Masters, McCord said, "The greens look so fast, I think they were bikini-waxed."

Why is the large tree in front of the tee on the seventeenth hole at Augusta called "The Eisenhower Tree"?

President Ike Eisenhower loved to play at Augusta National, but the large tree on the left side of the fairway became his personal nemesis. Ike used to hit a slice and would always aim down the left side of a fairway. On Augusta's 17th, his ball seemed to end up in the tree every time. It became such an annoyance to the President that he pleaded with Clifford Roberts to cut it down.

Since St. Andrews was the site of the beginnings of organized golf, why isn't the Royal and Ancient Golf Club of St. Andrews considered the oldest golf club in the world?

The Royal and Ancient is not the oldest golf club in the world. The Honorable Company of Edinburgh was established in 1744. Thus, the Honourable Company was in business ten years before the Royal and Ancient.

Why is there a World War I memorial placed near the 12th green on Turnberry in Scotland?

The land of Turnberry has particular sentimental value for those who fought in World Wars I and II. The course was turned into an airfield in both wars. The evidence of the airstrip can be seen along the 12th hole, and a memorial to the war dead of World War I was erected on a hill near the green.

The Rules

On May 14, 1754, the Honourable Company of the Royal
and Ancient Club was formed and developed thirteen
articles that have served as the basis for the rules of play
that we use today. The Rules of Golf command the
allegiance of the world's golfers. Few sports can boast the
intrinsic sense of honesty required by the game itself. In
what other sport do competitors call penalties upon
themselves without reservation? The Rules of Golf are
always, however, being tested by new situations, rubs of the
green and technological advances in equipment. The Rules
serve to keep the game as a sport defined by skill and based
on fairness to all who tee it up.

Why are there fourteen clubs?

Theoretically, if there were no limit to the number of clubs a player could have a club for every possible contingency and thus have an unfair advantage over the competition. The USGA and the Royal and Ancient agreed on fourteen because it represented a standard set of clubs—2- through 9-irons, a wedge, a putter and four woods.

Why do players drop a ball at an arm's length rather than over their shoulder as they used to do?

The modification in the Rules had several intents. While dropping a ball for relief, a player would often bounce it off of his shoulder or heel by accident, so that the ball landed outside the drop area. The drop over the shoulder also often caused players to toss the ball rather than drop it. By extending one's arm for the drop, the likelihood of the ball remaining in the intended drop area is increased.

Why is there a rule against grounding a club in a sand trap?

Rule 13-4 prohibits the touching of soil, sand or any living thing in a hazard as a means of preventing testing the texture and thereby gaining an unfair advantage. A hazard is considered a form of punishment for a stray shot. Testing the sand or soil would partially negate the effect of the "punishment."

Why is there a rule against "building a stance"?

If there were not a rule against building a stance a player could take measures that would certainly be unfair. For example, a golfer faced with a downhill lie could use a small pedestal or fill in the ground to make his stance level. Players could also use devices to help them push off their back foot. The rule is intended to make everyone play the course as intended.

Why does Rule 10 state that players who play out of turn in stroke play will be disqualified if their intent was to give an advantage to a player? What is the advantage?

The rule is intended to prevent two or three players agreeing to hit first in order to help someone. The scenario might go as follows: Two players are hopelessly out of the hunt in a stroke tournament. Their good friend Bob is only a few shots back with five holes to go. As a favor for their friend, they agree to hit before Bob. Bob is able to see what clubs were hit, how the ball travels in a wind condition and how it reacts upon landing. This type of behavior would be a serious breach of the Rules and a common sense of fairness and deservedly carries the penalty of disqualification for those involved.

Why do the Rules of Golf place so much emphasis on amateur and professional status?

The Rules of Golf have almost ten pages on the status of amateur and professional. The main emphasis is on fairness. It would not be fair for someone who derives his living from the game to play against those who play golf as an avocation. Much of the attention the Rules give to status is the definition of what constitutes being a professional and how one may apply for reinstatement as an amateur.

Why is there a difference between a water hazard and a lateral water hazard in the Rules?

If a ball lands in a water hazard the Rules call for the player to drop a ball behind the water hazard and to keep the spot at which the ball crossed the water hazard between the player and the hole. In many cases, such as a wide river or ocean inlet, it is not practical or possible to do this. Lateral water hazards are marked with red stakes, and a ball should be dropped within two club lengths of the point where it entered the hazard.

Why can't a player go to an adjoining sand trap, take a swing to test the consistency of the sand, then step into the trap in which his ball lies and play it?

This practice would not be in keeping with the spirit of the game and is prohibited by the Rules. Rule 13-4a states that "a player shall not... test the condition of a hazard or similar hazard."

Why is there a rule against using foreign materials on a golf ball?

Rule 5-2 was written with the intention of preventing a player from gaining an unfair advantage by using a substance that could change the flight characteristics of the ball. For example, a ball sprayed with a slippery substance does not have as much sidespin, so that hooks and slices can be avoided. Such actions, not dependent on golfing skill, are outlawed.

Why do some scorecards have a figure called "slope" on them?

Handicaps may vary from course to course, depending on length and difficulty. Every player should have a USGA handicap expressed in strokes and a fraction of a stroke as well as the handicap that he carries at his home course. If a player travels to a new course he or she may convert the USGA handicap into a course handicap by using the Course Handicap Table on the scorecard or posted in the clubhouse which is known as the "slope."

Why are pin placements made as they are in tournaments?

There are no specific rules in regard to the location of pins. Greenskeepers, however, use some general guidelines of fairness and common sense in cutting the holes. At most PGA tournaments the holes are usually cut six on the left, six on the right and six in the middle so as not to favor players who prefer to draw or fade their shots into the green. Greenskeepers also keep the ground flat around the cup and consider the type of shot required to get the ball close.

Why is the term "through the green" used in the Rules?

The term "through the green" is used repeatedly in the Rules to denote the entire area of the course with the exception of the teeing area and putting green of the hole being played. There is no reference to the terms "fairway" and "rough" in the Rules of Golf. The word "green" was synonymous with a golf course in the early days of golf.

Why are tournament officials concerned with time in golf?

The Rules of Golf mention time several times. Although advocates of the game love the lack of a clock, in tournament golf time comes into play: a ball is lost if it is not found within five minutes; failure to start on time may result in disqualification (though if the player arrives within five minutes he may be penalized two strokes in stroke play or lose the first hole in match play); and finally there are penalties (two strokes in stroke play, loss of hole in match play) for undue delay on the course.

Why can't a caddie hold an umbrella over his player while he putts?

Rule 14-2 (assistance) states: "In making a stroke, a player shall not accept physical assistance or protection from the elements." The rule is intended to prevent one player who has special equipment or help over someone who does not. This rule, as are most rules, is designed to restrict competition to golfing skill and not the result of gimmicks or special advantage.

Why can you move a hazard stake that interferes with your swing when you cannot remove an out-of-bounds stake in a similar situation?

A hazard stake is an obstruction. Whether it is movable or not depends on how it is installed. Objects defining out-of-bounds are not obstructions and cannot be removed.

Why is it difficult for a touring pro to revert back to amateur status?

All professionals who seek to become amateurs must apply to the USGA for reinstatement and then undergo a two-year waiting period. However, the Rules of Golf state that "players of national prominence who have acted contrary to the Definition of an Amateur Golfer for more than five years normally will not be eligible for reinstatement."

Why are the rules-making meetings called "quadrennial conferences"?

The Rules of Golf are formulated in a joint effort between the Royal and Ancient Golf Club of St. Andrews and the United States Golf Association. Delegates from the two associations meet twice a year to review proposed changes. The rule book, however, is published only every four years, thus the name "quadrennial" is affixed to the conferences.

Why is a stroke counted for a player who swings and misses the ball because the wind blew it off the tee before the clubhead arrived?

Rule 11-2 states that a ball may be reteed if it falls off the tee while addressing it. However, once a player makes a stroke—"a forward movement of the club made with the intention of fairly striking at and moving the ball"—it is indeed counted.

Why don't the touring pros use binoculars to survey the area for their shots?

Rule 14-3 prohibits artificial devices and unusual equipment. Such items as range-finders and survey equipment would greatly take away from the spirit of the game and give too much prominence to technology over golfing skill.

Why do the Rules allow practice on the course before a match play event but not stroke play?

According to Tom Meeks, director of Rules and Competitions for the USGA, there are no specific reasons why you can practice in the one case but not in the other. In fact, the note at the end of Rule 7-1 permits the Committee to reverse this rule. Mr. Meeks goes on to explain that the main reason why practice is permitted in match play is that there are only two players. In stroke play the numbers would be so large that practicing on the course could be a big administrative problem, and the maintenance crew might not be able to complete its work.

Why is so much emphasis placed on club design in the Rules of Golf?

Five very specific pages in the Rules of Golf detail the permissible design of clubs in order to keep the game one of skill rather than one of technology. The flight characteristics of a golf ball can be greatly influenced by such design modifications as the width between grooves on an iron, the mass of the clubhead, flex characteristics of a shaft and the material of an insert into the clubface. The basic idea is to preserve the game of golf as a function of a player's skill and not the result of advanced technology.

Why do many pros hold their clubs out of the grass in the rough as they address the ball?

It is legal to ground your club anywhere on the course except in a hazard. However, if the ball moves after you have taken your address, there is a one-shot penalty. To address the ball under the Rules you must 1) take your stance and 2) ground the club. Many top players hold the clubhead a few inches from the ball so that technically they have not addressed the ball. Should the ball move in this situation, there is no penalty.

Why was croquet-style putting outlawed?

Rule 16-1e prohibits standing astride or on the line of a putt. Croquet-style putting enjoyed a brief period of popularity when Sam Snead used it to cure his "yips." The croquet style, however, was never a traditional golf stroke, and never considered a fair stroke. Additionally, a player would gain a distinct advantage by being able to sight directly down the line of a putt as compared to the traditional manner of putting. Rule 16-1e was put into effect to preserve the traditional and inherent fairness of the game.

Why do most players feel it is difficult to play to their assigned handicap?

The USGA's system for computing a handicap does not measure the player's actual scoring average but rather his/her potential. The handicap is based on the last 20 rounds played but only the lowest 10 are taken for use in computing one's handicap.

Why can't players tamp down spike marks on the green?

There have been several explanations for this Rule. Firstly, tamping down spike marks might allow a player to get an advantage by creating a small "path" along his or her line while pressing down the marks. Another reason is that with numerous spike marks, the pace of play at all levels would be slowed down greatly as players tamped down all marks along their lines.

   More and more players, including the professional tour players, are using spikeless shoes that eliminate spike marks altogether and make the greens smooth for everyone.

Why was it that, in the original Rules of Golf, there was one that stated, "You must tee your ball on the ground"?

This rule seems to have been made to prevent golfers from using bushes or shrubs and making a baseball-like swing. This type of teeing the ball was said to be used by Germans playing the game *Kloven*.